MOMENTS

MADE FOR YOU BY...

THIS BOOK IS DEDICATED TO THE GREATEST, FUNNEST, SILLIEST, KINDEST, AND THE AWESOMEST MOTHER THERE EVER WAS.

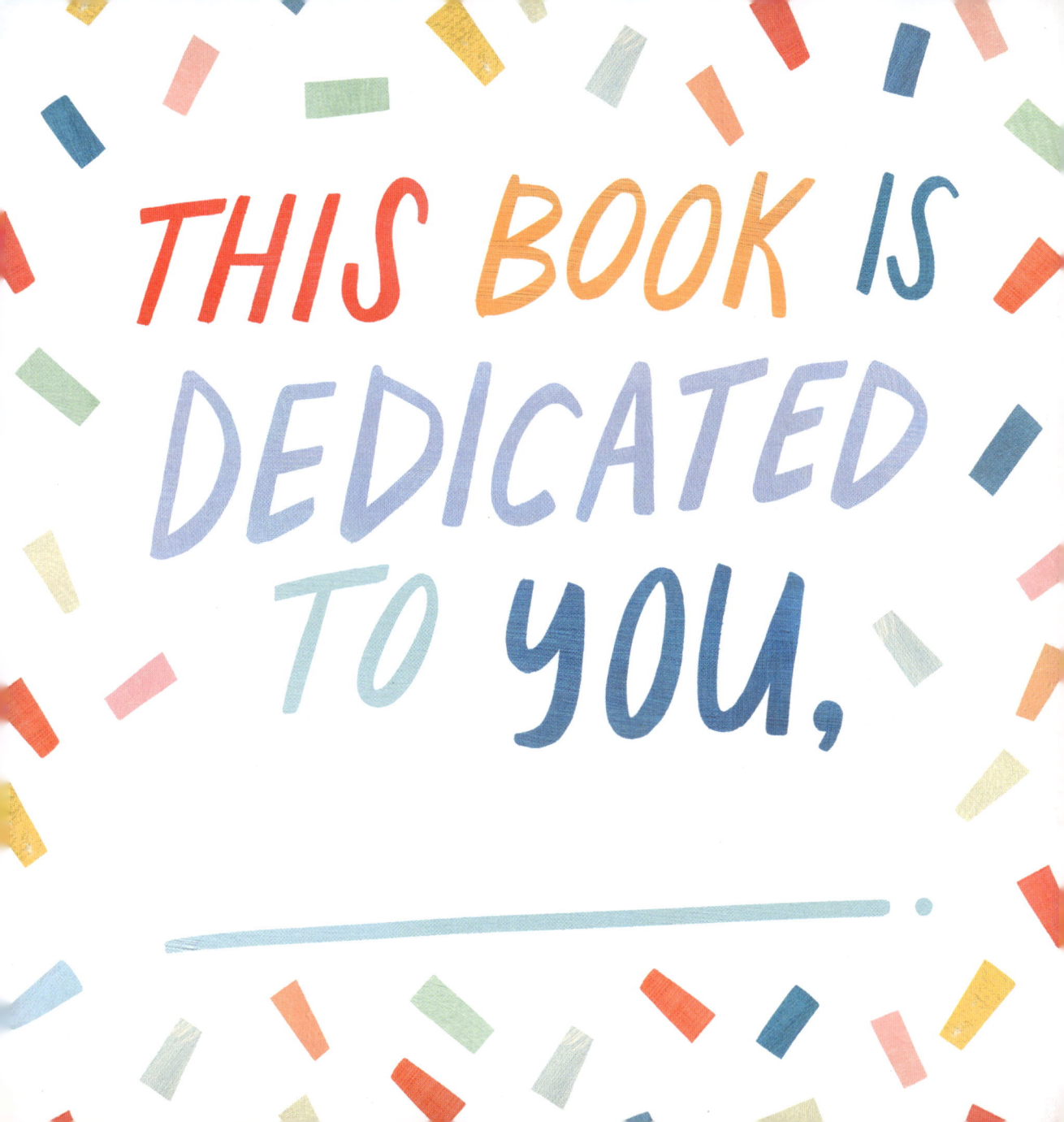

THE FIRST TIME I SAW YOU SMILING DOWN AT ME,

I PROBABLY THOUGHT

SHALL I
COMPARE THEE TO
A SUMMER'S DAY?
YES,

AS YOU ARE _____
AND _____ AND _____.

MOTHER, MOM, MADRE, MAMA, MAMMA, MA, MUM.

BUT TO ME YOU'LL ALWAYS BE

_____ .

EVERY TIME
I NEED TO
KNOW HOW
TO _____
_____,
I CALL YOU!

HMMM.
VINTAGE?
NOPE.
CLASSIC?
CLOSER.
YOU ARE
MORE LIKE

_____

_____

GOOD MOMS
LET YOU LICK
THE BEATERS...
GREAT MOMS
....
.................!

BUT

THAT ONE TIME YOU

_____

_____

_____

WHEN I WAS A KID
MADE ME SO MAD
THAT I THOUGHT
I'D NEVER TALK TO
YOU AGAIN!

YOU WERE RIGHT.

· ·

WAS **DEFINITELY NOT**
A GOOD IDEA. I FOUND
THIS OUT THE HARD WAY!

EVERY TIME I HEAR

_____

OR SEE

_____ ,

I ALWAYS
THINK OF YOU.

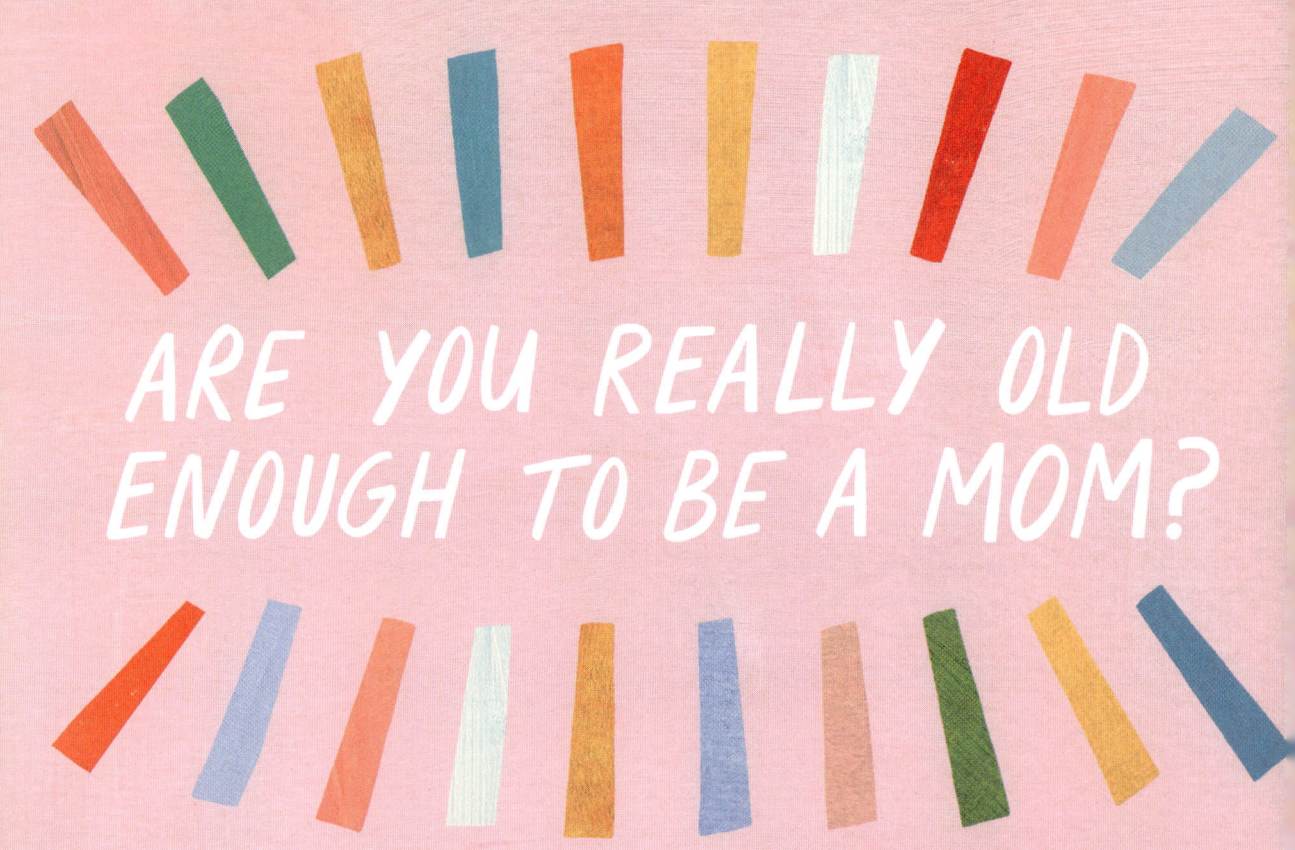

ARE YOU REALLY OLD ENOUGH TO BE A MOM?

I DIDN'T THINK SO. BUT IF YOU WERE...

THE ONE THING YOU
WOULD HAVE LEARNED
THE MOST BY NOW
IS THAT KIDS ARE

------------------------------------.

BUT YOUR KID(S)
ARE BY FAR

------------------------------------.

MOTHER

/ˈməT͟Hər/

1 A PERSON WHO IS ....
BEYOND ....

2 A LOVELY ....
WITH A BRAVE ....

3 MADE UP OF A WHOLE LOT OF

....

MIXED WITH A WHOLE LOT OF

....

4 SOMEONE WHO'S NEVER A

....

AND ALWAY'S A ....

ONE DAY THEY'LL WRITE A BOOK ABOUT YOU. THERE WILL BE ___ PAGES, ___ ILLUSTRATIONS OF ALL YOUR FAVORITE THINGS,

_____ PHOTOGRAPHS OF

_____,

AND THEY'LL TITLE IT

_____.

I'LL BE THE FIRST
TO BUY IT!

IF I SAW A

· ·

WALKING DOWN THE
HIGHWAY WEARING A

· ,

YOU WOULD BE THE
FIRST PERSON I'D CALL!

REMEMBER THAT TIME YOU AND I

_____

_____?

I LOVED THAT DAY!

YOU GET THE ULTIMATE **MOM** TROPHY FOR

_____ .

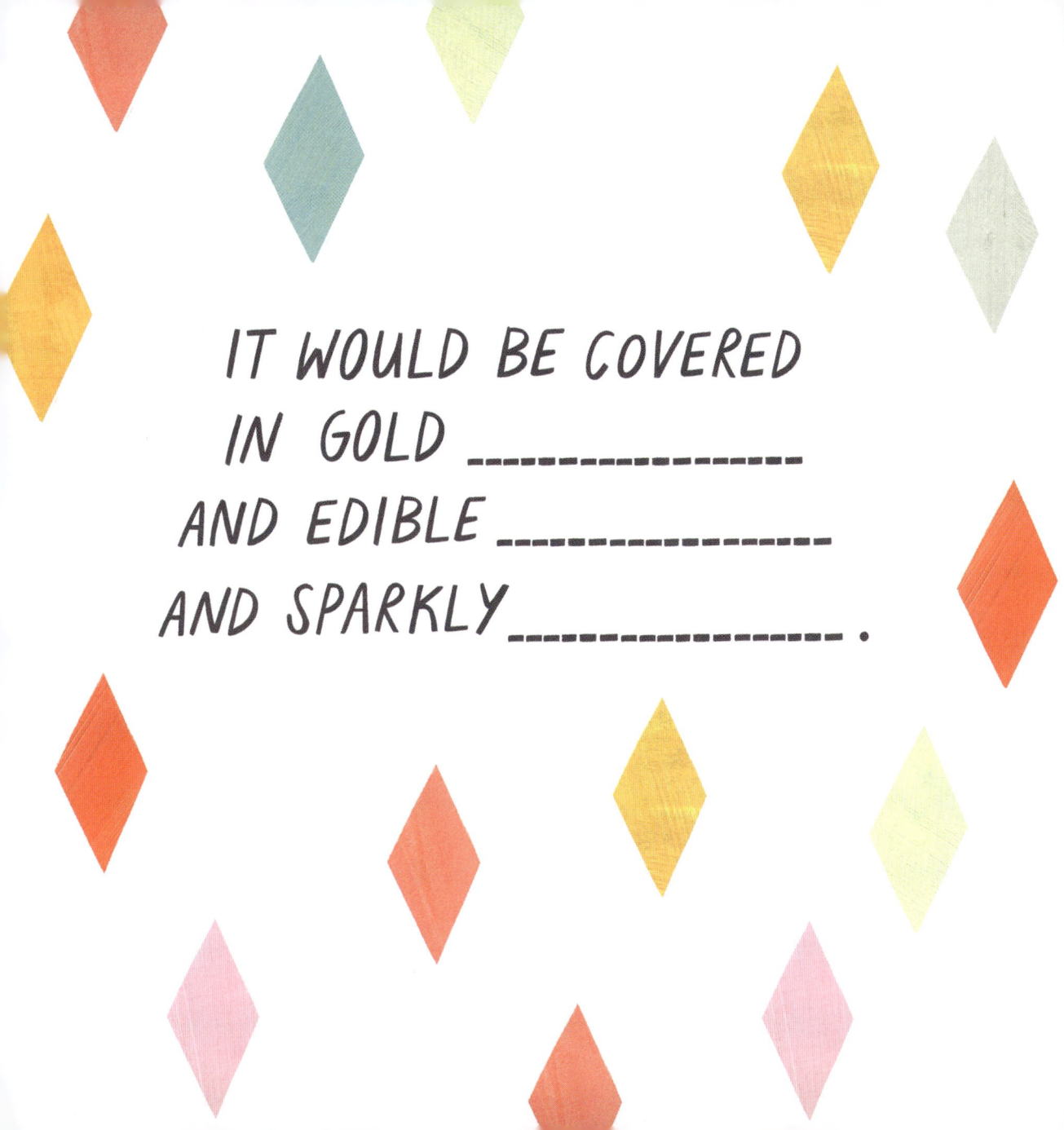

IT WOULD BE COVERED
IN GOLD _____
AND EDIBLE _____
AND SPARKLY _____.

THE CRAZIEST OUTFIT
I'VE EVER SEEN YOU
WEAR WAS ....
....
....

THE FUNNIEST THING I'VE EVER SEEN YOU DO WAS

_____

_____

I THINK I CAN SAY I KNOW YOU PRETTY WELL:

NEVER FAILS TO MAKE
YOU HAPPIER THAN A
UNICORN SLIDING DOWN
A RAINBOW.

YOUR FAVORITE
POWER TOOL IS A

_____ ,

WHICH MAKES
SENSE BECAUSE
YOU ARE SO

_____ .

....

IS HOW YOU FEEL ABOUT
MARSHMALLOWS IN CEREAL,
AND YOU'D SELL YOUR
SOUL FOR ONE LAST

....

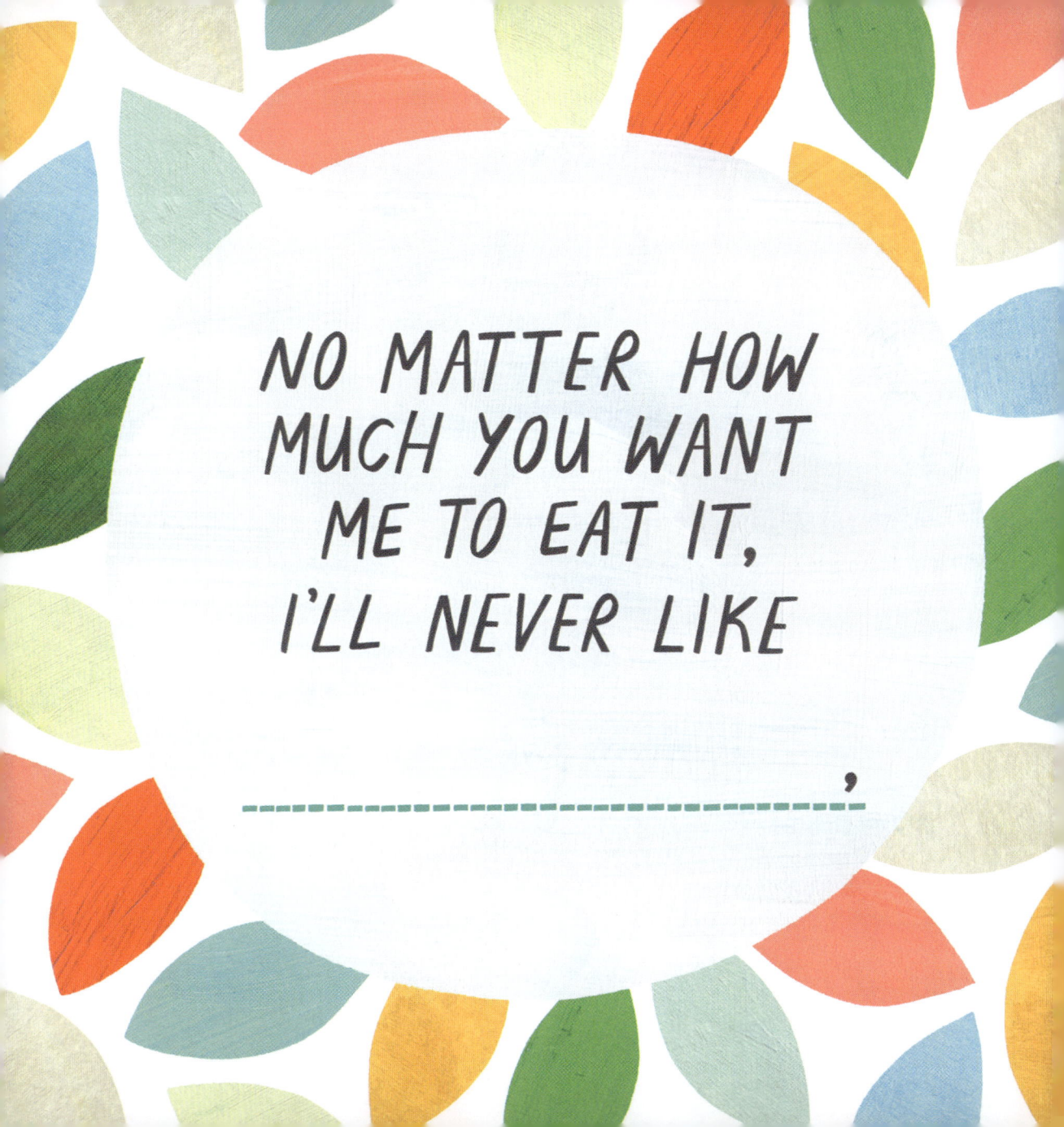

NO MATTER HOW
MUCH YOU WANT
ME TO EAT IT,
I'LL NEVER LIKE

_____ ,

EVER!

IN FACT, I'D RATHER

THAN EAT

!

DESPITE IT BEING MIDNIGHT, I'D STILL CALL YOU IF I NEEDED

WE LAUGHED
TOGETHER WHEN

------------------------!

AND WE CRIED
TOGETHER WHEN

------------------------.

I'LL ALWAYS
BE YOUR
WINGPERSON

FOR ....
AND ....

MOM, YOU'RE THE

_____

TO MY

_____.

WE HAVE $10 TO SPEND AT THE DOLLAR STORE. I'D DEFINITELY GO FIND_____

AND THEN I'M SURE
I WOULD FIND YOU
DOWN THE

_ _ _ _ _ _ _ _ _ _ _ _ _

AISLE!

IF YOU WERE MADE
INTO A MONUMENT,
YOU'D BE
_____ FEET HIGH

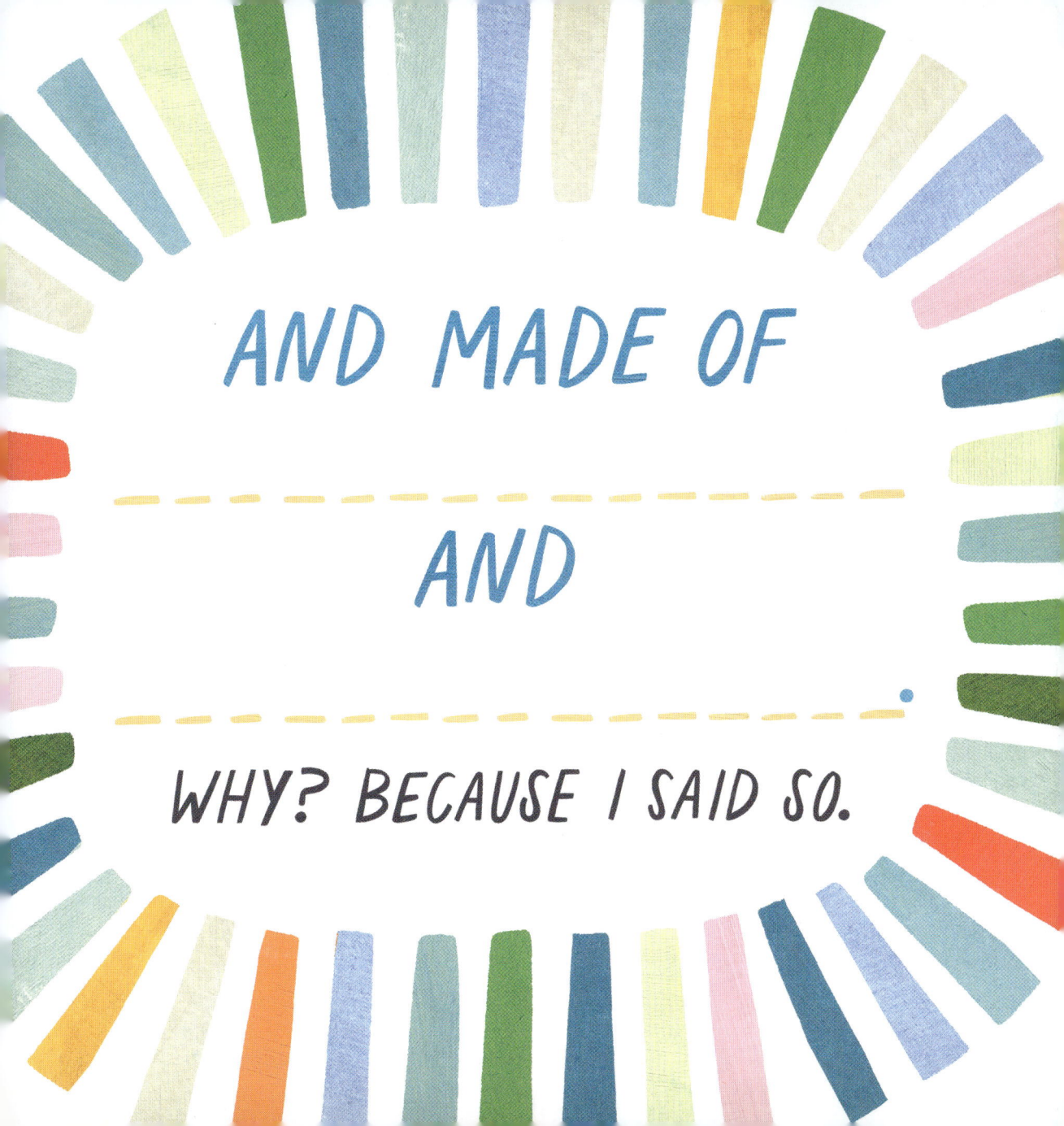

AND MADE OF

————————————————

AND

————————————————

WHY? BECAUSE I SAID SO.

MOMS SAY THE STRANGEST THINGS!

FROM, "MAY THE BIRD OF PARADISE FLY UP YOUR NOSE" TO

"

....

....
                                                                              "

....

AND NOW I'VE FOUND MYSELF SAYING SOME OF THE SAME THINGS!

HERE ARE A FEW MORE PHRASES THAT YOU ALWAYS SAID, AND NOW I DO TOO!

(THIS IS MY FAVORITE!)

(REALLY, I'M NOT SURE
THIS ONE MAKES SENSE!)

(I SWORE I'D NEVER
SAY THIS ONE! ALAS...)

I WAS IN SO MUCH TROUBLE WITH YOU THAT TIME I

....

....!

I THOUGHT YOU'D NEVER
FORGIVE ME!

BUT YOU DID, OF COURSE.

IF YOU HAD A
REALLY FLUFFY PUPPY,
YOU'D PROBABLY
NAME IT GOUDA.
OR MONKEY.
OR MAYBE

_____ .

AND IF WE FOUND A BABY PANTHER ON THE SIDE OF THE ROAD IN A DESERTED TOWN ON OUR WAY HOME FROM _____, WE'D PROBABLY NAME IT _____.

I LAUGH EVERY SINGLE TIME
I THINK ABOUT THAT TIME WE
.... !

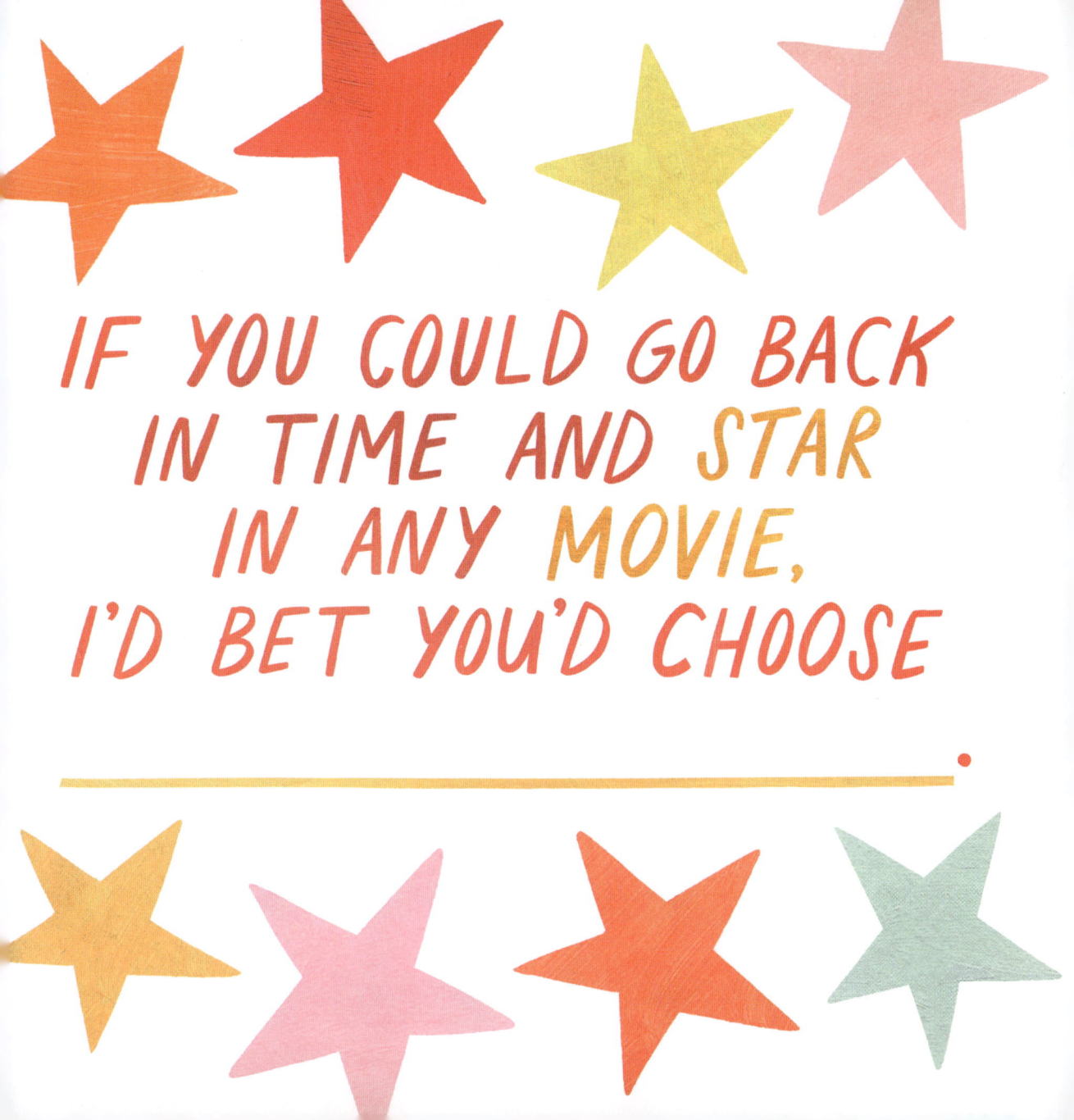

IF YOU COULD GO BACK
IN TIME AND STAR
IN ANY MOVIE,
I'D BET YOU'D CHOOSE

YOU'RE WEIRD FOR

_____ .

I'M WEIRD FOR

_____ .

AND WHEN WE

.... ,

WE'RE SUPER WEIRD
TOGETHER!
BUT I SAY NORMAL
IS VASTLY OVERRATED
ANYWAY!

MOTHERS ONLY GET 1 DAY,
BUT SHARKS GET A WHOLE WEEK?!
YOU ALSO DESERVE A WHOLE WEEK
OF ENDLESS ATTENTION AND
.... !

I SECRETLY BELIEVE THAT ALL MOMS ARE REALLY _____ IN DISGUISE.

JUST AS ISHMAEL SAID IN
MOBY DICK, "I KNOW NOT ALL
THAT MAY BE COMING,
BUT BE IT WHAT IT WILL,"
I KNOW YOU'LL GO TO IT

_____ .

BECAUSE YOU'RE

_____ ,

THAT'S WHY!

AND BECAUSE
YOU HAVE
1/4 PATIENCE,
1/2 UNDERSTANDING,
1/4 WIT, AND AN
ENTIRE BEING
FULL OF

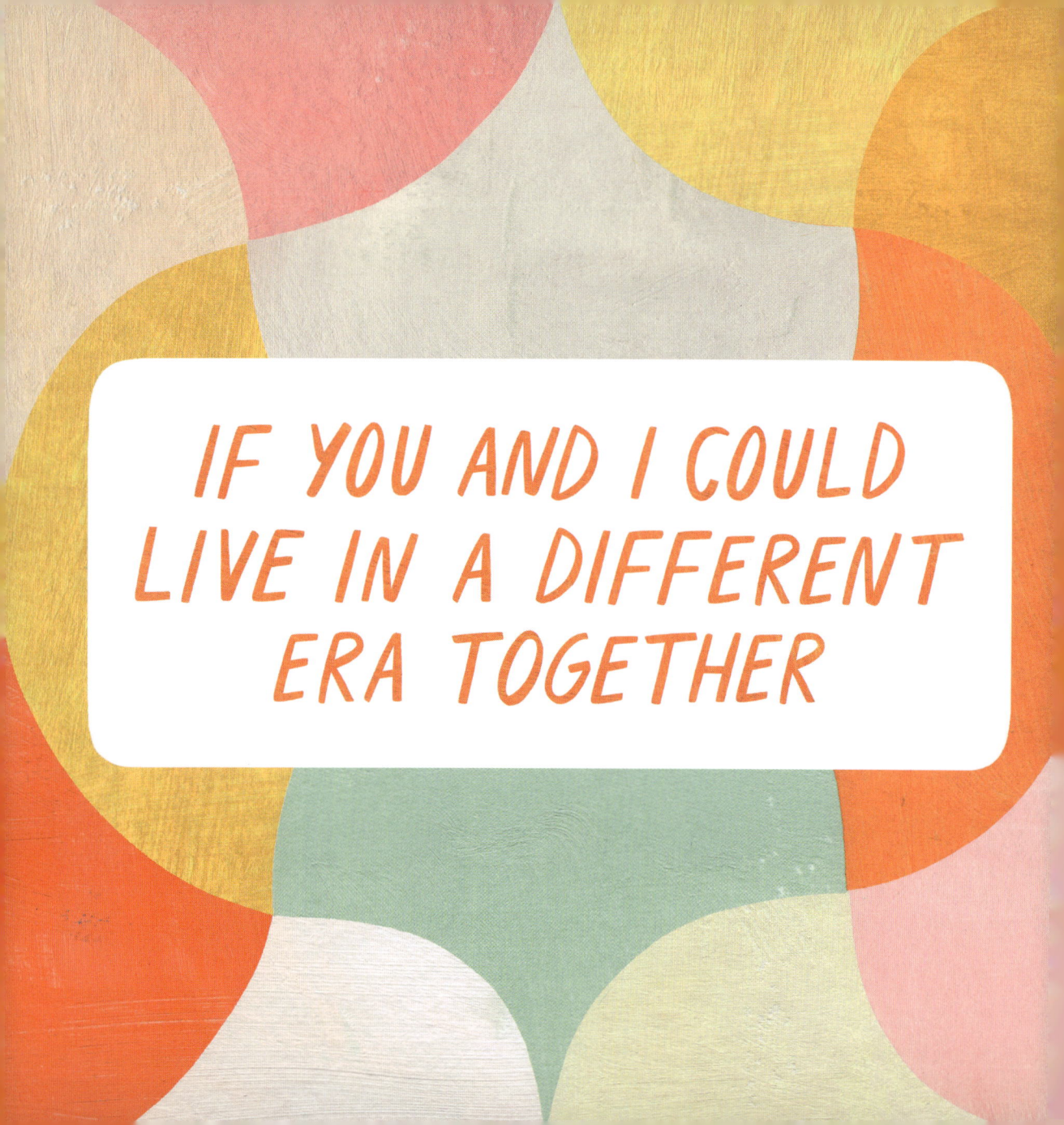

I THINK WE SHOULD LIVE IN

·····································,

BECAUSE

·····································

·····································

I THINK IF YOU WERE TO BE AN ANIMAL, YOU WOULD BE A _____.

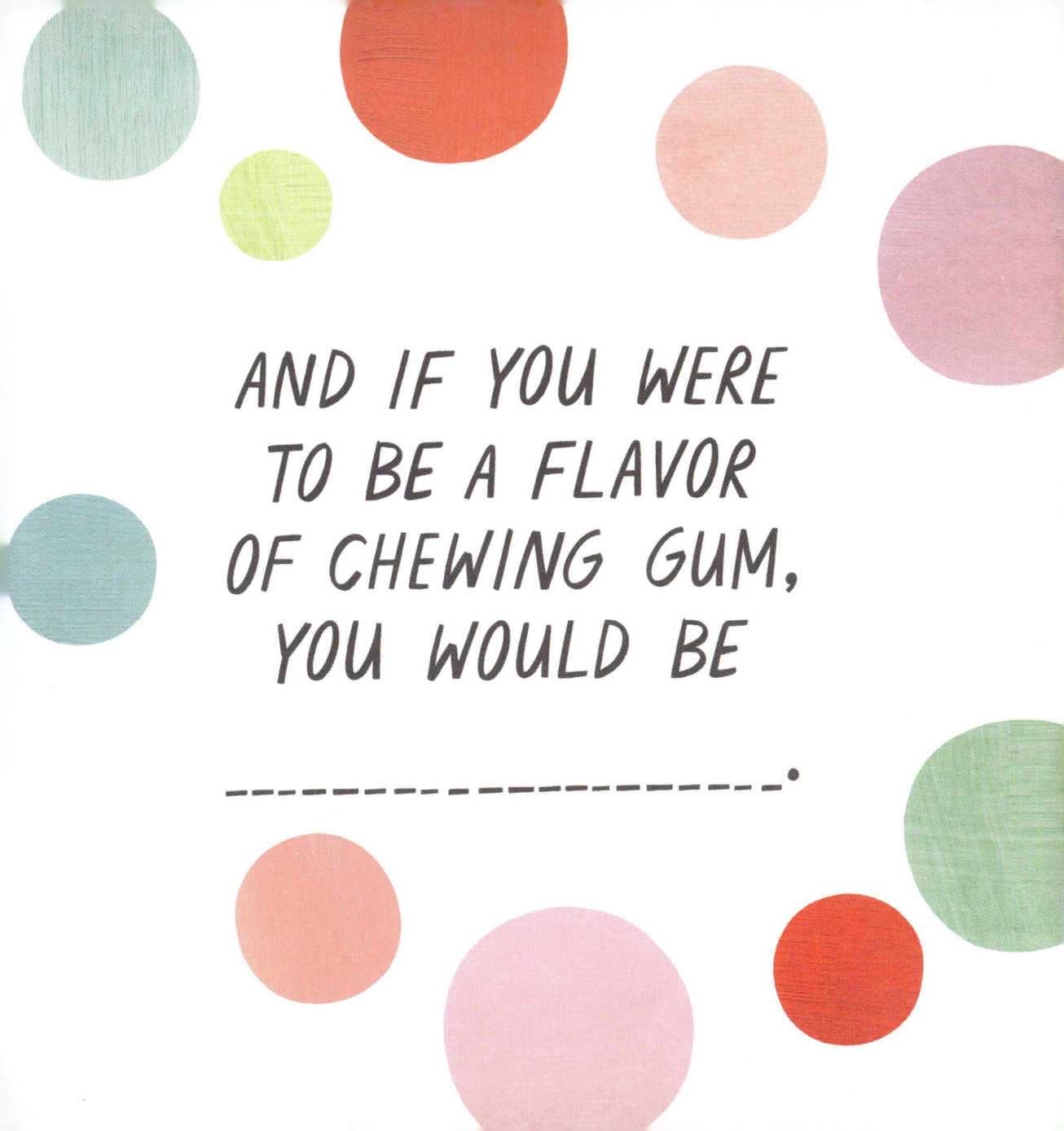

AND IF YOU WERE
TO BE A FLAVOR
OF CHEWING GUM,
YOU WOULD BE

_____.

IF YOU'D GO
TO JAIL
IT'D BE FOR

_____.

IF WE WERE THERE TOGETHER IT WOULD BE BECAUSE

------------------------------------ .

JUST HOW IT'S
IMPOSSIBLE TO
DESCRIBE WHAT
WATER TASTES LIKE,
I WOULDN'T BE
ABLE TO DESCRIBE
HOW YOU

_____

_____

TO ANYONE ELSE!

BECAUSE
YOU JUST HAVE TO SEE IT TO BELIEVE IT!

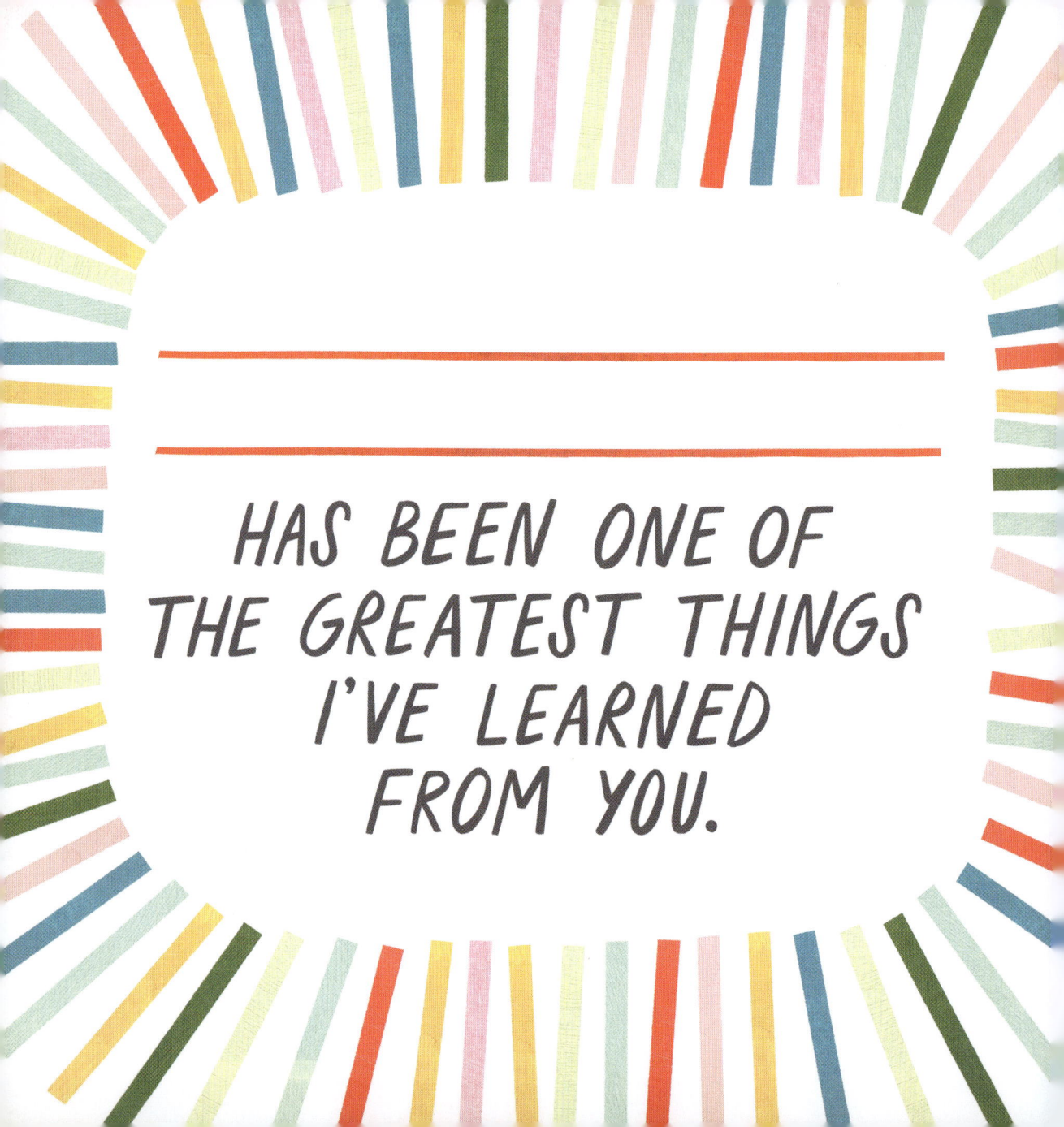

HAS BEEN ONE OF
THE GREATEST THINGS
I'VE LEARNED
FROM YOU.

I KNOW YOU LOVE ME BECAUSE YOU ALWAYS PUT UP WITH MY

_____

_____!

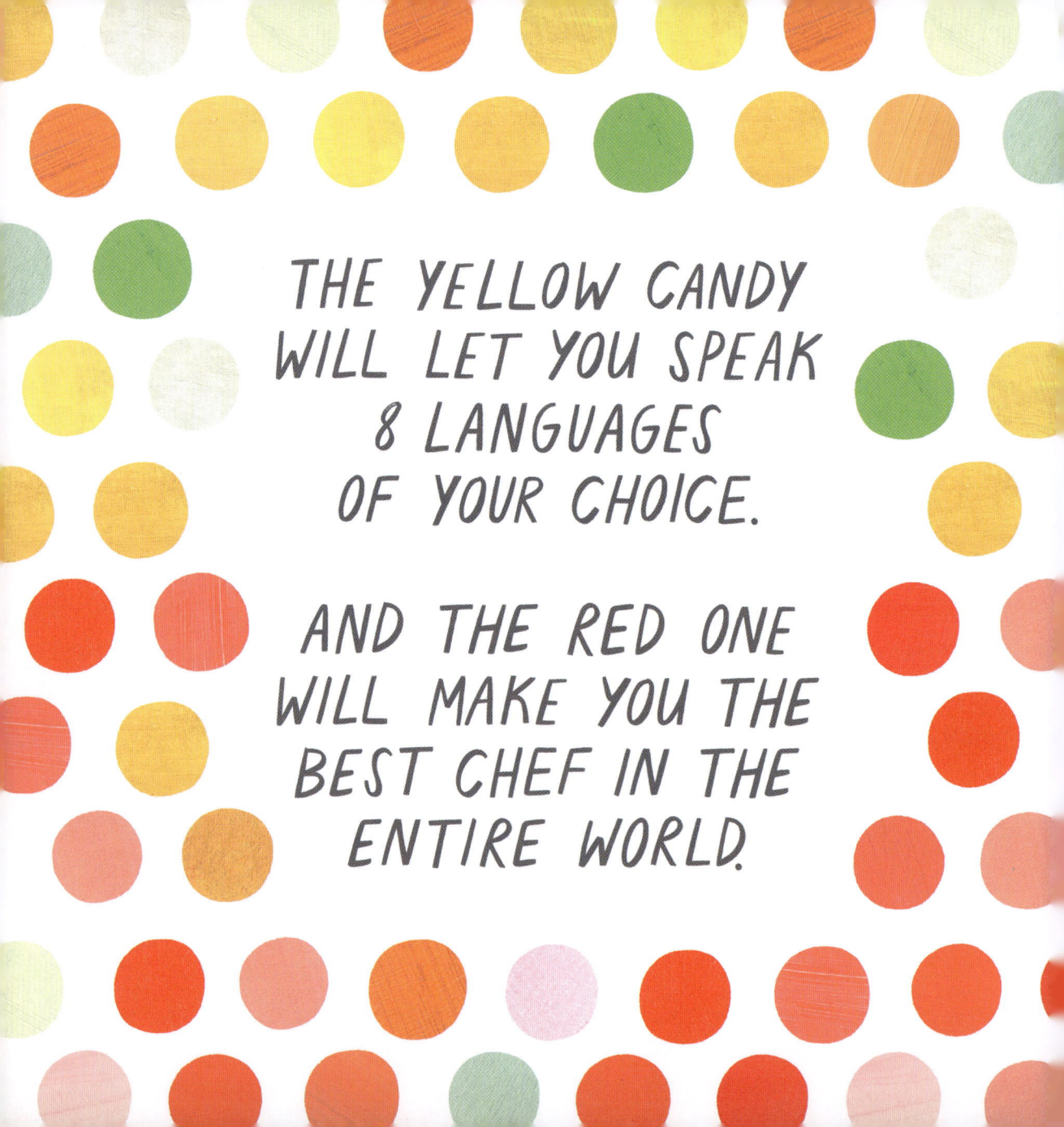

THE YELLOW CANDY
WILL LET YOU SPEAK
8 LANGUAGES
OF YOUR CHOICE.

AND THE RED ONE
WILL MAKE YOU THE
BEST CHEF IN THE
ENTIRE WORLD.

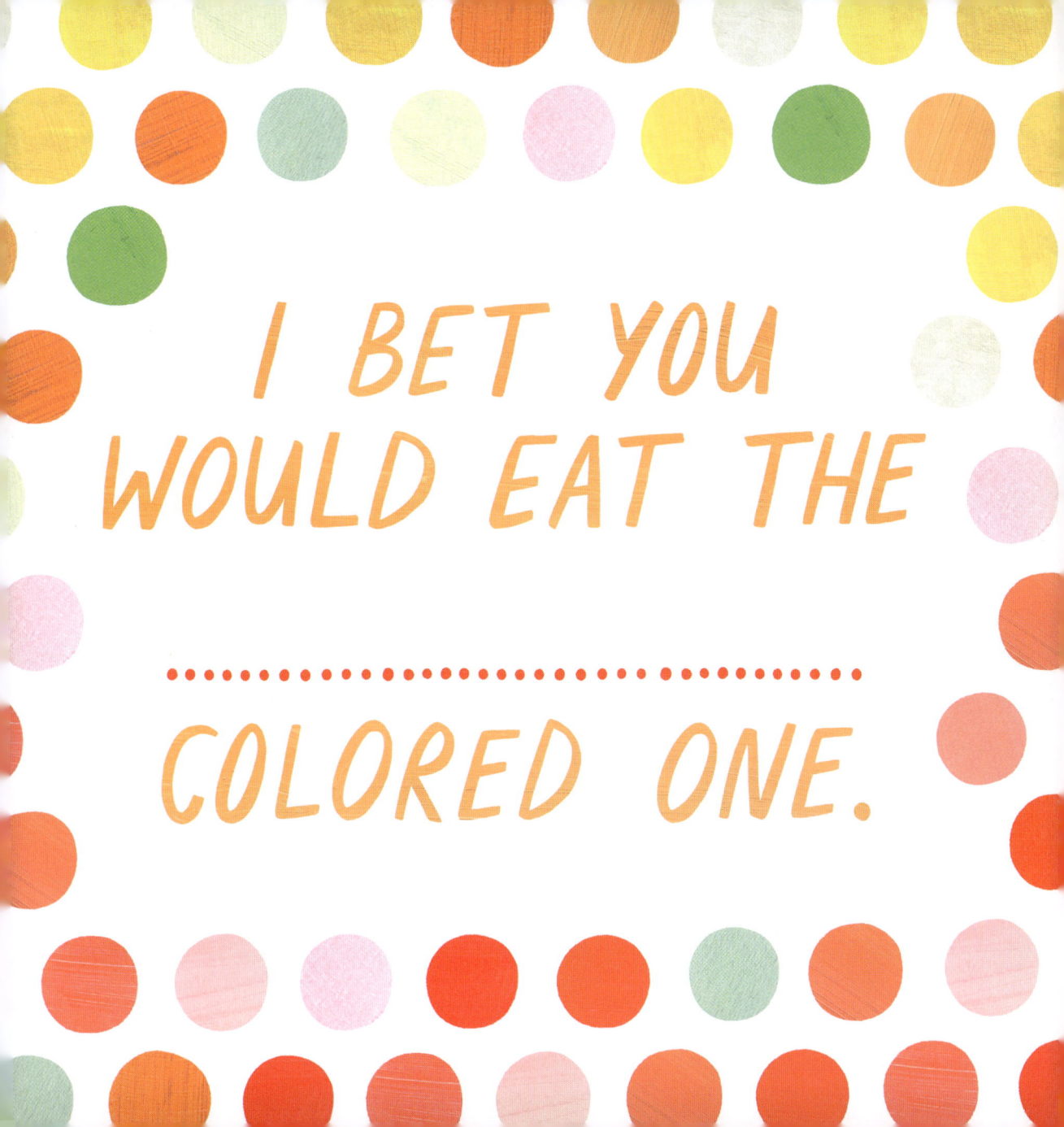

I BET YOU WOULD EAT THE

....

COLORED ONE.

YOU'D BE THE
_____-FLAVORED
CUPCAKE IN MY
LEFT HAND. AND THE
_____-COLORED
CUPCAKE IN MY RIGHT.

IF YOU COULD PICK ONE
MYTHICAL CREATURE TO
BE REAL, TO LIVE WITH
YOU AT HOME FOR THE
REST OF YOUR DAYS,

I THINK YOU WOULD CHOOSE A

_____

I'D MOST DEFINITELY WANT A _____

TO BE REAL!

IF YOU AND I COULD GO
ON A FOUR-MONTH-LONG
VACATION TOGETHER,
YOU'D SAY WE SHOULD FIRST
GO TO...:
AND THEN AFTER WE WENT
THERE, I WOULD TAKE
US TO....................................,
BECAUSE I KNOW YOU
LOVE IT THERE TOO!

BUT WE'VE BOTH NEVER BEEN TO

SO, LET'S GO THERE NEXT!

NOW,

THINGS TO PACK FOR THIS TRIP...
I KNOW YOU COULDN'T LIVE
WITHOUT YOUR _____.
AND WE'D HAVE TO MAKE
SURE WE PACKED ALL YOUR

_____.

THEN I'D GRAB_____
FOR YOU BECAUSE
I KNOW YOU'D FORGET.
AND DON'T WORRY ABOUT

_____.

IT/HE/SHE/THEY (CIRCLE ONE)
WILL BE THERE WHEN YOU
GET BACK!

YOU ARE SO MANY THINGS ALL AT ONCE. BUT YOU ARE THESE ABOVE ALL!

MY FAVORITE PERSON
TO WATCH .... WITH!

OUTSTANDING WHEN YOU........................
I COULD WATCH YOU DO THIS ALL DAY!

THE ONLY PERSON IN THE WORLD
WHO CAN DO ....

HILARIOUS WHEN YOU TRY TO

....

EFFORTLESSLY ....
HOW DO YOU DO IT??

REASSURING. WHENEVER I FEEL
........................, YOU ALWAYS HELP
ME TO FEEL ....

IF I DIDN'T HAVE YOU AS THE MOST AWESOME **MOM** THAT I DO, I'D CHOOSE YOU AS A

_____.

BASICALLY, I LOVE YOU
MORE THAN A WHOLE
TRAIN CAR FULL OF

_____

AND MORE THAN 80 THOUSAND
SHOPPING CARTS LOADED
WITH _____.

THANK YOU, MOM,
FOR BEING MY

_____.

GIBBS SMITH
TO ENRICH AND INSPIRE HUMANKIND

24 23 22 21 20   5 4 3 2 1

Published by
Gibbs Smith
P.O. Box 667
Layton, Utah 84041

1.800.835.4993 orders
www.gibbs-smith.com

Designed by Melanie Mikecz

Printed and bound in China
Gibbs Smith books are printed on either recycled, 100% post-consumer waste, FSC-certified papers or on paper produced from sustainable PEFC-certified forest/controlled wood source. Learn more at www.pefc.org.

ISBN: 978-1-4236-5451-3